HOUSE
HUMANS

# CONTENTS

# HOUSE
# HUMANS

*Daniel MacIvor*

PLAYWRIGHTS CANADA PRESS
TORONTO • CANADA

*House Humans* © Daniel MacIvor Copyright 1992
**Playwrights Canada Press**
215 Spadina Ave., Suite 230 Toronto, Ontario CANADA M5T 2C7
Tel: (416) 703-0013 Fax: (416) 408-3402
e-mail: orders@playwrightscanada.com
http://www.playwrightscanada.com

**Playwrights Canada Press** acknowledges the support of The Canada Council for the Arts for our publishing programme and the Ontario Arts Council.

*Cover design:* Randy Gledhill
*Photographs:* Mike Lo
The punctuation in this book adheres to the author's instructions.

**Canadian Cataloguing in Publication Data**
Brooks, Daniel, 1958
    House Humans
A play
ISBN 0-88754--521-1
I.MacIvor, Daniel,1962-   II Title
PS8553.R658H58  1996    C812'.54        C96-931998-3
PR9199.3.B76H47  1996

First edition: 1992 (Coach House Press) 2nd printing,1996 Playwrights Canada Press.Third printing, 1999. Fourth Printing, 2005.
Printed and bound in Winnipeg, Manitoba by Hignell Book Printing.

# Foreword by Daniel MacIvor

The cover of this book reads "by Daniel MacIvor" which is, in fact, not entirely the case. *House* began as a title and a dozen pages of notes and disconnected stories which I brought to Daniel Brooks. Over the course of a few weeks, he pushed and cajoled and asked me questions and I whined and fought and tried to please him, and together we came up with something resembling a play. It was the continued development of the text and performance over the next two years which brought us to the version you now hold. We made the play together and, although I was officially responsible for the "words", the structure and "story" were elements of a collaborative effort.

I mention this for two reasons: one, because Daniel Brooks' contribution to *House* has often been overlooked, and understandably since the sole performer here is the "writer" and few people really understand what a director does anyway, and secondly, because it is necessary to understand fully the process of development of this piece if one is to understand its power.

The thing about working in the way we do — where responsibility is not based on "job description", and ownership of an idea is not only irrelevant but impossible — is that the work remains alive. By "alive" I mean that we never allow the 'word' to become holy and untouchable. *House* is about performance rather than interpretation of a text. Meaning? The drive, the narrative line, the power of the piece is found in the relationship between the performer and the text; there is, in a very real sense, no "internal" monologue — the only monologue is the one on stage, on view. This is also to say that there is no superfluousness here — no imagery or wordplay for its own sake. We have been diligent and rigorous in trying to avoid a theatrical consciousness other than the theatrical self-consciousness of Victor.

When the play was first performed, there was much talk about its innovative nature — I was surprised by this because it did not seem innovative to me to have a character speak to an audience, indeed, it seemed to me as old as the first notions of theatre — night-time storytelling around the fire. But what people were engaging in was the seeming lack of pretense in the direct address; there is no huge effort required for the audience members to suspend their disbelief, instead they are faced with an almost unnerving authenticity — Victor is being honest, he is trying to tell the truth — no deceptiveness, no clever tricks. A note that Daniel Brooks has continued to give me through our years of working on these solo performances is "fail miserably". Sometimes Victor's jokes don't work, sometimes his stories don't go anywhere — there are no apologies necessary — the more miserably he fails the more thrilling it is for the audience.

What this speaks to, for anyone considering performing this piece, is the need for the actor's unwavering presence on the stage. I will not say "in the character" because that is ultimately irrelevant; to even think in those terms, "in character", immediately indicates a distance between the actor and the character and this thinking can create such a profound and troubled relationship between the actor and this supposedly distant character that there is little room for any relationship with the audience. Rather, here, we use the text as a map and the stage and the room around it as the physical universe of the journey — it is left to the actor only to be present on stage in his own fear, anger, and uncertainty.

Whenever we would talk about *House* to outsiders, Brooks would describe it as an explosion of self — and that is as far as we ever went in discussing the piece metaphorically; we never became bogged down with what things meant — they meant what they meant to Victor — Victor was who he said he was, whatever he said was true.

For us it was important that the metaphors were not worked consciously into the play, that they grew organically inside our concerns, not "presented" per se, but planted as seeds to sprout in the imagination of the audience members, in their dreams, and as they moved through their lives after having met Victor. Victor, this strange man created by two men and now offered to you.

As for *Humans,* I look at this collection of fables, parables, and fairy tales and see very much the kind of material that began the process toward Victor and *House.* I encourage you to read them aloud, dramatize them, change the voices and discover the simple, specific world from which they all commonly emerged. And in many ways they are all stories told by Victor since they and he share a deep belief in the fragility of the physical and the power of the spirit.

Daniel MacIvor
Toronto, 1996

DANIEL MACIVOR was born in Sydney, Cape Breton in 1962. He studied Theatre at Dalhousie University in Halifax and at George Brown College in Toronto. He is an actor, director, producer, writer, and artistic director. His theatre company, Da Da Kamera, has been actively producing his work since 1986. His other plays include *Somewhere I Have Never Travelled, Yes I Am and Who Are You?*, *See Bob Run*, *Wild Abandon*, *Never Swim Alone*, *This is a Play*, *Jump*, *The Lorca Play*, *2-2 Tango*, *Here Lies Henry* and *The Soldier Dreams*.

MacIvor has been nominated five times for the Chalmers New Canadian Play Award: in 1988 for *See Bob Run*, in 1990 for the collective creation *White Trash, Blue Eyes*, and in 1991 for *Never Swim Alone*, *2-2 Tango* and *House* which won the award. In 1995, *House* has was made into a film by Laurie Lynd. MacIvor has been touring nationally and internationally with *Here Lies Henry* which won a Fringe First award at the 1996 Edinburgh Fringe Festival. He is also a film and video maker whose projects include: "The Fairy Who Didn't Want to be a Fairy Anymore" (with Laurie Lynd), "Parade" (with Brad Fraser), and "Permission". He currently lives in Toronto.

# HOUSE

*House* was first workshopped as part of the Research & Development Program at Toronto's Theatre Centre. The play subsequently premiered at the Factory Theatre Studio Café in Toronto in May 1992, produced by Da Da Kamera in association with Factory Theatre.

Performer and Writer: Daniel MacIvor
Director and Dramaturge: Daniel Brooks
Stage Manager: Anne Driscoll
Sound: Greg Rhodes
Set Construction: Alex Fallis

*House* was remounted in the Mainspace of Theatre Passe Muraille in Toronto in April 1992.

Performer and Writer: Daniel MacIvor
Director and Dramaturge: Daniel Brooks
Stage Manager: Anne Driscoll
Sound: Dominic Giovinazzo / Pipco

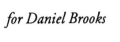

*for Daniel Brooks*

*Centre-stage a chair*
*Off left a small clamp lamp*
*Spotlight on chair*
*House lights to black. We hear the sound of huge*
*applause, yelping, hooting, bravos*
VICTOR *enters*
*He sits in the chair. Stands. Regards the chair. Walks*
*front with the chair. Throws it off the stage. Exits*
VICTOR *re-enters with another (identical) chair. Sets*
*it down. Sits on it. Stands. Regards the chair. Walks*
*front with the chair. Throws it off the stage. Exits*
VICTOR *re-enters with another (identical) chair. Sets*
*it down. Sits on it. Relaxes*
*With a gesture he cuts the sound of the applause*
*He snaps his fingers and stage lights come up full*
VICTOR *looks angry and rolls a tiny invisible ball*
*between his thumb and forefinger*
*Stops*

VICTOR  Hello. Thank you for coming. Thank you for
not going someplace else. Thank you for not staying

home and watching teevee. Thank you for coming here.

[**VICTOR** *looks angry and rolls a tiny invisible ball between his thumb and forefinger. Stops*]

I hate it when they don't do that. Might as well say hello. We're all just a room full of people so, hello.

[**VICTOR** *looks angry and rolls a tiny invisible ball between his thumb and forefinger. Stops*]

I made that up. I did. For group. GROUP! My group: a bunch of fucked-up people sitting around on little wooden chairs in the basement of our Our Lady of Perpetual Hypocrisy Church being all fucked-up sitting in a circle smoking cigarettes drinking coffee and at the apex of the circle—and I know a circle doesn't have an apex okay but this is not a perfect circle so it has an apex—and at the apex of our circle is our leader: Mister 'Call-Me-Joe' (and I won't: call him Joe). You can tell he's our leader because he's the only one in natural fibres, and you gotta respect him for that. Unfortunately his brain isn't present, his brain went missing in 1967, went on a trip with Lucy in the Sky with Diamonds never came back. And all us fucked-up people sitting around him smoking cigarettes drinking coffee and being all fucked-up. That be Trish: pills; Harvey: booze; Joyce: booze; Mrs.

Davidson: stuck her head in an oven; be Jennifer: co-dependency thing with her boyfriend won't go out without him; be Jennifer's boyfriend: nothing wrong with him he's just with Jennifer; be Stew: weird; that girl with the glasses and the split ends who hasn't said anything in three months 'cept there's nothing wrong with her but there is TRUST ME! And then there be me. And what's my problem? GUESS!

[VICTOR *looks angry and rolls a tiny invisible ball between his thumb and forefinger. Stops*]

They got Creative Therapy in group. The idea of that is you make things with your hands and your brain is busy keeping your hands busy so it doesn't have time to EXPLODE! Making things useful things, like, ceramic bears to put cookies in or those little Canadian maple leafs made outa burnt-out matchsticks or candles rolled in sand or macramé—MACRAMÉ! the last bastion of macramé is group—macramé owls with big button eyes you hang on your wall ... OR lampshades made outa popsicle sticks—you know how many popsicle sticks it takes to make a lampshade? THOUSANDS! Poor Mrs. Davidson she wanted one of those popsicle-stick lamp-shades so bad she had to get her stomach pumped. She ate all those popsicles all by herself in the bathtub—and only grape! Why? She came outa that bathtub looking like a

big birthmark. She had to go to the hospital to get her stomach pumped, she was big as a 7 Eleven, she was big as a house.

HOUSE! [*stands and thrusts his arms up in victory*]

Lampshade came out not looking too bad if you like that sort of thing—BUT I DON'T! So this one week Mister 'Call-Me-Joe' (and I won't: call him Joe) he says to us:

'Hey Guys …'

Guys, or:

'Hey Gang …'

Gang or guys he's always calling us. Makes you feel like you should be on a field trip to a museum or something holding onto a rope.

'Hey Gang, next week for Creative Therapy I want you to create something at home and then bring it in and show it to the group.'

Okay. So I do. I go home, make it up, come in, sit down, do it.

[**VICTOR** *looks angry and rolls a tiny invisible ball between his thumb and forefinger. Stops*]

Mister 'Call-Me-Joe' (and I won't: call him Joe) says:

'Hey Victor man, what wuz that you were doing?'

I say, being angry and alone and rolling a tiny invisible ball between my fingers, waddaya think ya jerk!

He says:
'Hey Victor man that's not creative.'
Why not?
Yes it is so creative. I should know. I CREATED IT!

[*Pause.* VICTOR *walks front and lifts his pants legs*]

I'm not wearing any socks. And I'm not going to tell
you why I'm not wearing any socks because that is part
of the mystery of me.

[VICTOR *returns to his seat. He looks angry and rolls
a tiny invisible ball between his thumb and forefinger. Stops*]

My buddy Stew from group he thought it was creative.
He said it gave him a feeling—and that's what's creative!
It gave him a feeling! If it gives you a feeling it's creative.
You don't have to be able to hang it on your wall for it to
be creative, you don't have to use glue for it to be creative,
if it gives you a feeling it's creative, and my buddy Stew
said it gave him a feeling. He said it gave him a feeling of
when you're trying to get to sleep at night and there's a
big ball of rubber on the ceiling and a spoon taking
scoops out of it and whiffing them at you, he says it's a
feeling you get in your teeth.
Stew's weird.

Now you might think that I'm weird but I'm not. I'm fucked-up. There's a fundamental difference between weird and fucked-up. You are born weird, you get fucked-up. You can't be born fucked-up or get weird. You have to be born weird. I'm fucked-up, Stew is WEIRD.

You want first-hand evidence of that you invite him to your place. You invite him to your place he will steal, even if you're his friend he will steal from you and not smart things either, stupid things, won't steal the teevee or the toaster or the quarters for the laundry, he'll steal stupid things like, steal the handles off your kitchen cupboards so you come home three o'clock in the morning want something to eat don't want to turn the light on … [*reaches for non-existent handle*] steal the thing out the back of your toilet that floats, he'll steal the round things you got on the bottom of the chairs in the living room so they don't dent the carpet, steal the receiver off your telephone! You leave him alone in a room with a telephone he'll take the receiver off the telephone put it in his pocket when he goes it's gone and what good's a telephone without a receiver and what good's it to him— can't sell it—what good's a receiver without a telephone. Unless of course Stew's been to your place! OR! This one week after group we're going for coffee Stew wants to stop off and get some gum cause he's off the butts … Don't mind if I do.

[**VICTOR** *looks for cigarettes, can't find any, tries to rally*]

Butts.
Coffee.
Group.
Stew.
Gum.
GUM!

We're going for gum. We're going for coffee after group Stew wants some gum so I say Hey let's go in this Variety Store because Variety is the spice of life—but no, Stew has to go in the Supermarket. Why? Because he's fixated on Supermarkets. Why? Because he likes the lighting, AND because he likes the dairy section because you can stick your head in a fridge and pretend to be looking for something. That's the other thing about weird people, they're always complaining they have hot heads because their brains are overworked from thinking about shapes and colours all the time. 'Shapes and colours shapes and colours the whole world's made up of shapes and colours.' IGNORANCE IS BLISS!

So I'm there in the gum section: 'What kinda gum you want Stew? Stew? Stew?'

But Stew's not there, no, he's in the dairy section, I gotta drag him out of the dairy section. So we get the gum we're standing at the cash waiting to pay there's this woman in front of us with a whole cartload full of process food with which she is going to go home and kill her family. She's got one of everything that's bad for you. Now she turns around she sees Stew with gum with me with nothing, she doesn't say anything. Does Stew say anything? NO!

Doesn't say:

'Excuse me lady I only got a pack of gum you got a whole cartload of stuff mind if I go ahead of you?'

NO! He just stands there while she takes out each and every package of poison puts it on the counter punches it into the calculator. I'm getting TENSE! So I take a trip which is something I do when I get tense. I look around for something to take a trip on and I take a trip. I see the bird on the box of Froot Loops in her cart—she's got THREE boxes of Froot Loops! So I'm on my trip: I'm sitting on the counter in her kitchen, I'm invisible, her two sets of identical triplet boys are sitting at the table, all six years old, she's on the phone, talking to her sister in Medicine Hat, the boys are starving, she throws a box of Froot Loops on the table, they rip it open, eating the Froot Loops dry, getting little pieces of cardboard caught in their throats and making those little coughs, she hangs up the phone throws the boys in the basement locks the door no wonder they got such bad eyes they're locked in the basement all day no wonder their teeth are rotted out of their heads they're eating dry Froot Loops!

## HOUSE

Okay. So I'm back in the Supermarket. And not a dent made in the cart! Why? While I was in her kitchen she ran off to aisle seven got another dozen packages of Ding-Dongs. I'm getting TENSE! So I do my calming action which I got from group which is counting to thirty very slowly on my fingers and thinking of waves used to be counting to fifty but it took TOO GODDAMN LONG! I get to twelve it's a tidal wave so I turn to the woman give her one of these: [*raps himself on the side of the head with his knuckles*] one of these: [*again*] on the side of the head.

'Hey is anybody home, is anybody home at all? That's the problem with this country there's nobody HOME!' SIGH Well, you woulda thought I shot her. PAUSE

Cops there, everything, and they're charging me with assault. Assault? With what? With this? [*two raps*] What's that? [*two raps*] That's a symbol. [*two raps*] That's a metaphor. They're charging me with assault with a metaphor … 'Stew back me up, Stew back me up, Stew back me up.' No. Why? Stew's gone! They're charging me with assault with a metaphor meanwhile the real criminal is fifteen blocks away with a mouth full of STOLEN Bubblicious! PAUSE

That's the world we live in welcome to it.

Couple of days later I catch up to Stew:

'You idiot!'

He says to me:

'Man you're weird.'

(ME!) And I gotta remind him one more time:

'Stew my friend Stew you are weird me I'm just
FUCKED-UP!'

[VICTOR *steps forward*]

A man goes to a fortune teller. The fortune teller tells
the man: 'You mus buy a hoose an move into dee hoose
unt say dere for vun yeer an den dis yeer vill bring for you
great sadness unt great joy!'

Well the man was very excited when he heard this
because up to that point his life had been plain and
unremarkable. And so the man finds a house, he buys the
house, he moves into it and stays there for one year. And
any time the phone would ring ... any time there was a
knock on the door ... any time a car would pull into the
driveway ... the man would prepare himself for great
sadness or great joy. And even though whenever the
phone would ring ... it was only ever a wrong number,
and even though whenever there was a knock on the door
... it was only ever a guy selling a vacuum cleaner, and
even though whenever a car would pull into the driveway
... it was only ever to turn around and go the other way
... the man would always remember 1987 as his best year.

[VICTOR *circles the chair suspiciously*]

[*calling off-stage*] MaryAnn!
[*tearfully*] MaryAnn.

MaryAnn used to be my third cousin then we got married now she's my wife. Ma introduced us. She had us both for dinner then she took me in the kitchen and told me: Marry your cousin. I thought she was nuts but later we're sitting around the tube watching the Shroud of Turin on 'Man Alive' and I look over at MaryAnn and the blue light of the Shroud of Turin on 'Man Alive' is dancing on her face and she looks over at me and goes: [*mouthing*] 'Boring.' 'Boring.' So I fall in love with her. MISTAKE! So we get married. MISTAKE! Why? Because I neglect to find out before we get married that the woman can't stand me. And why can't she stand me? You got two days? But the main reason of why she can't stand me is because of my job and it's not my fault it's my job it's just my job it's not my fault.

I was gonna be an engineer. But I'm not.

I was gonna be an engineer.

I was gonna be an engineer for two reasons. First reason of why I wanted to be an engineer was because engineers are the guys who figure out how to build things so they don't fall down. Figure out how to build the floor so the ceiling won't cave in, figure out how to build the ceiling so the walls won't bend. Now that is useful information, especially if you ever had anything fall on you.

The second reason of why I wanted to be an engineer was because THEY'RE SO FUNNY! Oh yeah, engineers are the guys who on April Fool's put a Volkswagen on the roof of the cafeteria or fill the Dean's office with liquid insulation. NOW THAT'S FUNNY! But it is to be *respected* because it's not a joke. It's not. Any idiot can tell a joke, I could tell a joke, but it's not a joke, it's a ... prank! Ah! And a prank! is to be *respected* because it involves COMRADERY! Ah! Comradery! I never had any comradery. Comradery was something I saw twenty-five yards away in a field with a bunch of guys and a ball. I never had any comradery. (If we had violins we'd play them.) You know, comradery, when you're a kid and you're gonna put a frog in a paper bag and set it on fire and throw it on somebody's doorstep, you gotta figure out whose doorstep, who's gonna catch the frog, who's not scared of frogs, who's gonna put the frog in the bag, who's not scared of warts, who's gonna set the bag on fire, who's not scared of getting burnt. You know comradery. And engineers are the most comraderistic people in the whole world and I always imagined that when they'd be doing their prank, they'd all be up in some office where they broke in late at night with a skeleton key and they'd be putting the photocopier in the water cooler then when they were finished they'd come down into the street being all quiet and happy and proud of their prank and the sun would be just coming up and they'd be saying beautiful poetic things to one another like:

'See ya tomorrow.'

'Call ya Friday.'

'Wanna go for breakfast?'

And that might not sound like poetry but it does if you never heard it and I never did.

I was gonna be an engineer but I'm not.

I clean septic tanks.

Of course I don't actually clean them myself. I work in the office. Millard's Sanitary Vacuum Service Office Worker!

Speaking of fashion: I prefer a slip-on shoe, we've discussed the socks, a polyester slack, an open-neck shirt, a sporty sports jacket, they say clothes make the man I wish they'd make the bed, I wish they'd make the money.

Money.

Mommy.

Mother.

Father.

Father!

My father was in the septic-tank business. He installed 'em. And he was a bit of a septic-tank hero because he saved a kid from drowning in a septic tank one time and so he had his picture in the paper and that and became a hero so that whenever you thought of septic tanks you thought of my father and whenever you thought of my father you thought of septic tanks. That happens with heroes. That's association. Like you think of war you think of soldier you think of cop you think of doughnut. Like that. And when my father left my mother to go and join the circus ... and that's another story, too long, no time, can't tell it ... she went into this deep depression and said the only way she would get out of it is if I went into the septic-tank business or became a priest and I said to her:

'Ma how can I become a priest I'm not a FAG!'

And I can say that because I was a fag in my last life, and I'm gonna be a fag in my next life, or hey I don't know ... talk to me after the show.

But it's not a show ... It's my life ... It's my [*stands and thrusts his arms up in victory*] HOUSE!

But you know what really burns me up? That was thirteen years ago I went into the septic-tank business, my mother's still depressed. Why? Because she won't live her own life she insists on living her life through me and if you were living your life through me wouldn't you be depressed! But I want to say to her, Ma get your own life, would you please get your own life! But she can't because then she would have to go out into the world and talk to people and admit that she's a human being and she won't admit that she's a human being, why? Because human beings are what? BAD! And they stink, well they must they sell enough deodorant. But us eh, we're not afraid to admit that we're bad and we stink are we!

Are we!

Are we?

[VICTOR *snaps his fingers. The stage goes black. He sniffs in the darkness. He snaps his fingers. Lights up. He is standing front*]

There was a man who had a house and every Wednesday night he would invite all of his friends over feed them dinner and then get drunk. And when he got drunk he would tell each and every one of his friends in a very loud voice in a very direct way exactly what was their problem. And then he would get drunker and tell each and every one of his friends in a very loud voice in a very direct way exactly what it was about them that made them one in a million. And every Wednesday night the house was packed because well to hear that you are one in a million how sweet it is to hear such words of love. And every Wednesday night the house was packed because everybody knew when the man told them what was their problem he was just drunk.

[VICTOR *pulls a piece of green plastic indoor / outdoor carpeting from his pocket*]

Does that look like *grass* to you?

[*He discards it*]

I've been with the company for twelve years. Twelve years at Millard's Sanitary Vacuum Service. That's one year for every desk in the office. That's six months for every fabric partition between the desks. That's one day for every day I had to hear Tom the guy at the next desk say: 'Well somebody's gotta do the dirty work ha ha ha.'

The immediate reality of my reality of my ... space would be me and my desk, be the frosted-glass office of the King of Millard's Sanitary Vacuum Service Mister Millard, be Brenda his personal and private secretary who is SO deluded she's been there three years and she's still looking for the elevator, and Brenda! we don't got an elevator!, be Tom the guy with the sense of humour like a head cold, then there be the big desk by the window, that be Andrew.

Andrew.

'Hey Sport ...'

(Sport.)

'Hey Sport, too bad you don't got a view ...'

He's got the view. He's got the view of the parking lot and St. Jude's School for Pubescent Girls across the street.

'... too bad you don't got a view, there's a little filly, there's a little filly now, wouldn't mind taking that little filly for a little t-t-trot around the t-t-track.'

Andrew's an idiot.

He went to University for two years he's got this tattoo

of an expression on his face, 'I been to University for two years,' who cares! He's always saying stuff like:

'If you knew anything about b-b-body language you wouldn't be sitting like that right now.'

He's an idiot.

But Millard loves him. Oh yeah. He loves him. Andrew's been there eighteen months. Eighteen months! What's that? That's not even a human being, you can't even form a complete sentence at eighteen months. But Millard says to him: 'Call me Jim.'

I been there twelve years he never told me to call him Jim. He's had Andrew out to his place to parties there. Mrs. Millard and Doris, Andrew's wife, joined a club together. Millard doesn't even know I'm married. Then Andrew goes on vacation two weeks comes back first day back comes into the office standing right in front of my desk Millard comes out of his office over to Andrew RIGHT IN FRONT OF MY DESK gives him ... a hug ... a *hug*. He *hugs* him. Why didn't he just pour hot wax in my ears. So I get depressed and when I get depressed I get angry and when I get angry I get depressed so to break the cycle I do something I haven't done in ten years I go looking for the old man. He's easy enough to find because he's still with the circus, he's got a little act worked up: Saddest Man in the World. So I find the circus I go to the gate tell the guy who I'm looking for he sends me down to the tent by the weight guessing. Get there big sign on the tent: 'SEE HERE SADDEST MAN IN THE WORLD' a line going in one side people all pink and dizzy from the tilt-a-whirl coming out the other side all grey and saaaaad. So I pay my money and get in line and so how it works is there's this wall with a hole in it and you stick your head in the hole and this is what you see: you see him and you think: What, he doesn't even look sad! He looks bored, this is a gyp, I want my money back. (Two bucks!) I want my money back. But then before you can look away his face goes all foggy and it's not him any more, it changes into an actual real flesh of you, but you when you were saddest saddest saddest ever in your whole life and you look and you think Oh My God I Can't Even Look At That so you look down at your feet but your feet aren't there cause your head's in a hole! so you look back and that's when it hits you … right there, in that secret of the secret, that place that you know you know but you're afraid to say you knew you knew, that place deep deep down deep deep deep deeper than your stomach deeper than your dreams deep down to that place that's just this round and wet on the inside that's that thing of 'Human beings aren't built to last,' that's that thing of all it takes for you to never ever be or ever have been or ever be again all it takes is: [*he brings his thumb and forefinger together and squashes the 'thing' making a tiny fart-like sound with his lips*] … That's worth two bucks.

[VICTOR *plays 'Amazing Grace' by putting his head back, plugging his nose and banging on his throat with the side of his hand creating the sound of bagpipes. After a few lines he stops and weeps. He continues. Midway he stops*]

Ah you know how it ends.

[*He approaches the edge of the stage conspiratorially*]

I know it's a theatre.
I do.
I know it's a theatre. I know it's a stage. I know it's a chair. I know it's a light.

[*He snaps his fingers, a bank of coloured lights comes on behind him*]

I know it's a light.

[*He snaps his fingers, coloured lights out*]

I know you're a house.

[VICTOR *snaps his fingers. House lights come up. He smilingly starts down off the stage*]

Oh oh. Oh oh. Oh no. Here he comes! He's ruining everything! I thought this was a PLAY! Stop! Stop! Now you wish you stayed home to watch teevee eh, teevee doesn't get up and walk around behind you, don't have to turn your head to watch teevee, never get a sore neck from teevee.

Nice theatre eh?

[*In the original production at the Factory Theatre Studio Café* VICTOR *began to make disparaging remarks about the theatre.* 'Nice if you like clean, nice if you like process cheese.' 'They wouldn't even give me a key, what were they afraid I'd invite Stew over? Don't have to worry nothing stupid enough to steal here, everything's very smart here.' *At the back of the theatre was a bar,* VICTOR *approached the bar and got out a glass of water, then standing by the fire exit:* 'I wanted to do the whole thing here in front of these doors but they wouldn't let me. Why? Fire regulations. Okay then how about a little campfire on-stage. No. Why? Fire regulations. They're crazy for fire regulations here. They're dying to have a fire to see if all the regulations work.' *He then returned to the stage*]

'Oh thank God he's back up there!'
Okay here's something.

[*He weeps theatrically*]

Acting!

They give awards for acting. Really. They do. Best Liar. Thank you very much. Best Written Lie. Thank you very much. Best Directed Lie. Thank you very much. YES! I know all about awards because I won one once.

[*He snaps his fingers. House lights out*]

I did. I won …
One.
Two.
Four.
Eight.
Late.
Work.
Sell.
SELL!

'Salesman of the Month.' I won Sanitary Vacuum Salesman of the Month and I don't remember what month it was but it was at least twenty-eight or maybe as many as thirty-one days and either way that's a lot of days to be best. And I was. And it wasn't in-office either. It was the Sanitary Vacuum Umbrella Organization and that takes in everything Sales, Installation,

Service, everything. I didn't even know the organization existed until I got the letter but hey I wasn't gonna argue. Salesman of the Month. As soon as I got the letter I get it all worked out in my head how it's gonna be night of. Night of me and MaryAnn take a cab down to the Ramada Inn where the awards are being held. (Take a cab cause I'm on the booze then. Don't drink and drive.) Get there walk into the Ramada go to Reception, 'Excuse me where are the awards being held?' she goes 'Oooo' points us off to the meeting room walk in the place is filled with people sitting at these long tables with white paper tablecloths drinking tomato juice all looking at us thinking: 'That's him.' and 'Isn't she lovely.' I'm pleased, she's beaming. Sit at the head table have our hot turkey dinner and as many rye and gingers AS I WANT they call my name I get up receive my plaque with my name and my picture on it make a speech about my father the septic-tank hero the crowd is warmed by my reminiscences, some people are crying, everybody claps, I with my wife on one arm my award under the other leave, walk out of the Ramada Inn and begin my new happy life.

WANNA BET!

Turns out night of is MaryAnn's Girls' Night Out ('Lingerie party sorry can't make it.') Fine, I go by myself. Take a cab down, driver takes me the long way around, fine everybody's gotta make a living. Get there nobody knows anything about any awards spend twenty minutes

looking for the room finally find it level two basement.
Fine. Walk in there's about a dozen guys sitting around
talking about septic tanks. Fine. Turns out dinner is hot
turkey *sandwiches*. Fine. Turns out … it's a *cash* bar. Fine.
Turns out the whole thing is put on by the Amway people
and they do a big demonstration of Amway and explain
how we should get out of the septic-tank business and get
into Amway. Fine. I get my plaque it's got my name
spelled wrong and a picture of ANDREW! Fine. Turns
out I don't get to make a speech because everybody
there's getting Salesman of the Month Award. Fine.
After we all go out to this strip club watch some skinny
blonde woman take her bra off on a plaid blanket and
throw up. Fine. I get home MaryAnn's sitting in front of
the tube I say:

'MaryAnn …'

She says:

'I'm watching this okay.'

It's a show about ALGAE! FINE! So I sit down I ask
myself a question. I ask myself: What's Wrong With Me?

Yeah yeah I know you all got an answer to that but I'm
not asking you I'm asking me and that is an important
point in a person's life when you can ask yourself a
personal question like that and I'm asking myself: What's
Wrong With Me?

So I get a dictionary I look up 'me':

Me: objective case of I.

Okay, look up 'I'.

I: subjective case of me.

Objective case of I. Subjective case of me. Objective case … Subjective case … AND I REALIZE! The problem's not with ME! The problem's not with I! The problem's with … the case! THE CASE! YES!

CELEBRATORY MUSIC PLEASE!

[*Loud electric guitar music à la Jane's Addiction or the like.* VICTOR *dances in short sharp movements then suddenly after about fifteen seconds makes a gesture to cut the music. Silence*]

So I am going to change my life.

And I'm not going to join the Y. Why? That's what everybody does when they want to change their life, join the Y. Why? What? So that I can build my body up so strong I'll never get out of it? No thank you. And I'm not going to leave my wife. That's what everybody else does when they want to change their life. I am not going to leave MaryAnn because I tried that and it was a nightmare in Technicolor. This one time I leave MaryAnn because we were getting all these invoices in the mail from *Swingles* magazine made out to 'Veronica, Mistress of Discipline,' no thank you, I leave. I pack up a little suitcase I go to Stew's place, knock on the door, Stew's girlfriend Darlene opens it takes one look at me with a suitcase: 'Nooooo way!' SLAM! That's fine, it's her prerogative to not stand me because she thinks I'm a fucked-up influence on Stew because she knows how weird he is and you gotta respect her for that. Also that Christmas party two years ago and we were SO both drunk ... but that's another story too long no time can't tell it, so I leave I go to my sister's place, lucky for me my sister can stand me. She's got a little bit of a problem though, she's got this thing with annulments. She's had five. It's easy for her to get them because she used to go out with this bisexual guy Dave who was a priest and now he's a bishop so she just calls him up:

'Oh Dave it's just not working with this guy ...'

So Dave just does a ... [*bangs himself in the forehead with his fist*] ... annulled ... didn't happen ... annulled ... didn't happen ... didn't happen. Now that's a stroke of brilliance eh? The Catholic Church they're something else. What nine-year marriage? What six kids? Didn't happen! So anyway my sister's just getting her fifth annulment which is good for me cause she has space for me to stay at her place BUT ... She's got this dog. Now that doesn't sound strange that a person would have a dog but if you knew my sister, she was all her life totally neurotic paranoid petrified of dogs. She used to have this recurring nightmare when she was a kid about all these dogs in pantsuits ... too long no time ... but she would wake up screaming, 'MY BONES! MY BONES!' But now she's got this dog, and this dog is not a normal dog, this dog is huge … HUGO she calls him … and Hugo is huge, this dog is big as a barn, this dog is big as a house.

HOUSE! [*stands and thrusts his arms up in victory*]

And my sister is big as a bug, big as a minute. So I think this is strange so next day I got group, I go in they're all playing Word of the Week and I hate Word of the Week so it comes to me for my turn I say … Hey … and I tell them about my sister and Hugo the dog and Mister 'Call-Me-Joe' (and I won't call him Joe) he says:

'Hey Victor man I think it's obvious what your problem is.'

Oh yeah hotshot what's my problem?

And he says:

'Hey gang, you wanna let Victor in on what his problem is?'

And every one of them at the same time, even that girl who hasn't said anything in three months says:

'You're jealous of the dog.'

Great.

I'm jealous of a dog.

GREAT ANOTHER PILE OF SHIT TO CARRY AROUND WITH ME FOR THE REST OF MY LIFE I'M JEALOUS OF A DOG!

But no I'm not. I'm not jealous of a dog because there is no dog, I annul it! I go back to my sister's place stay there with her and no dog. Easy.

THEN this one night I'm home early, I'm supposed to be home late but I'm not I'm home early walk up the stairs to the apartment all this racket coming from inside I walk in the place is filled with dogs. All these drunk dogs in the kitchen rooting through the cupboards and drawers, all these dogs lined up for the can, I go in the living room they got a red lightbulb in the lamp and all these dogs in couples all over the place, this Lionel Richie music is playing and in the corner is my sister slowdancing with Hugo the dog! NO THANK YOU! I'm on my way out I almost get killed trying to break up these two Irish setters fighting over the last of the paté and I'm trying to explain to them that hey guys the fridge is filled with paté but that doesn't matter they can't open the fridge they got no THUMBS! So I leave this nightmare ... and I go to my mother's place, which may be a stupid move but hey this is serious, I'm thinking about a divorce, this is serious stuff here I gotta talk to somebody about it. So I go to my mother's sit down she's sitting in front of the tube as per usual. The teevee's always on there, it's like a dialysis machine, you even look at the remote she goes into a seizure, but I got to talk to somebody! So:

'Ma.

Ma.

Ma?

Ma?

Ma!

Ma!

MAAAAAAAAAAAAAA!'

Nothing.

Okay then:

'Ma, I'm gonna get a divorce from MaryAnn.'

ZING! She's on me, she says:

'If you get a divorce from your wife you will spend an eternity in hell.'

Oh yeah.

I say to her:

'Oh yeah Ma, well that's okay, I already got my ticket, it's one-way and I'm taking YOU WITH ME!'

Well. Then there's this explosion. I'm out for ... well you don't know how long you're out when you're out do you cause you're out but I'm out for say two days. I come to, the room is filled with smoke and the smell of sulphur. Smoke clears a bit I look up on the ceiling ... MA! There's my mother on the ceiling. Her head is turned right around on her body, her eyes are big as turnips, her tongue is hanging out of her mouth about three feet all pointy on the end lashing around the room slitting the curtains ... MA! catches me here on the arm, sixteen stitches, she's got all this Latin coming out of her mouth, steam coming out of her ears and her perm is curling and uncurling, curling and uncurling, curling and uncurling ... MA PLEASE! I'm trying to get her down. MA PLEASE! I'm there a week and a half trying to get her down off the ceiling and it's getting uglier because the place is filled with goats and I'm allergic so finally I relent … 'Okay Ma I'll go back to MaryAnn.'

Zip. She's back in the La-Z-Boy, Paid Promotional Programming on the tube, nothing happened.

So I am not going to leave MaryAnn.

And I'm not going to join the Y. Why?

But I know what I'm gonna do.

I know what I'm gonna do.

This is the part about the house.

In the lunch room.

Ground beef. Absorbine Junior sauce.

Sitting at my table. Brenda's off looking for an elevator. Tom's telling Helen Keller jokes to the coffee machine. Andrew and Millard at their table practically all over one another as per usual. I'm sitting there moving a cup back and forth. Something I do to help me think. Move an object back and forth very quickly so it becomes long and blurry. It helps readjust my reality. And I think: Yes. I'm gonna do it. I wait till Andrew goes to the can I get up go over to Millard. Standing there a minute before he notices me. He looks up.

[VICTOR *snaps his fingers. Light becomes a single red spot on him*]

hi Sir how ya doing good to see ya listen i saw your car

in the parking lot you got a wax job eh? looks great i got a wax job on mine last spring fifty bucks but it's worth it … ah listen i don't wanna take up too much of your time … but we got some work done on the place and my wife and i were talking … oh yeah years … MaryAnn … and we were talking and we thought … you know i been here twelve years and … yeah! … and we never sat down had like a dinner and i was thinking that maybe you might be interested in coming out to dinner … at my house …

And he hems and he haws and talks about his busy schedule and his nephew's wedding and I say:

please … Sir?

And he says:

[**VICTOR** *snaps his fingers. Back to normal stage light*]

'Yeah I'll come.'

A COUP! So I got two weeks till night of. I get my sister we go down to the bank she cosigns a loan, twelve thousand dollars. I get landscaping job on the front yard floodlights on the house, get new carpeting living room, hallway, stairs, get rec room finally finished, get all new fixtures in the bathroom … and a bidet!, get whole new gut job on the kitchen, ceiling, floor, brand new appliances … almond! I come down morning of night of the place is like a dream, it's like a place off teevee where the family sits around the fireplace playing board games, it's perfect … except the kitchen floor. Ran out of money workmen walked out waddaya gonna do. But that's okay, I'm late, I gotta leave, but it's okay because MaryAnn can do it! Go in the kitchen MaryAnn's sitting on a box of tiles talking on the phone. Sees me hangs up.

'Who were you talking to MaryAnn?'

'Nobody.'

… If I had a dime for every time MaryAnn was on the phone talking to nobody, leaving the house going nowhere or coming home after doing nothing I'd be a TRILLIONAIRE! But that's okay and I'm explaining to MaryAnn about how I'm late I gotta leave but how the tiles are so easy …

'They're easy …'

and they are

'They're self-adhesive …'

they're self-adhesive

'They're black and white …'

black tile white tile black tile white tile black tile white tile easy.

'Hey MaryAnn don't even have to know your colours just the difference between black and white ha ha …'

MaryAnn goes for the phone.

'Who ya calling MaryAnn?'

'Nobody.'

MARYANN I AM DOING THIS ALL FOR YOU!

She gets up comes over to me standing very close I can

smell her hair ...

Then I go on this trip ... This is long long ages ago, haven't thought about this in years, we're at this party, MaryAnn's sitting in this group of people she's telling a story, I'm standing apart from them, can't hear what she's saying but I'm watching, and everybody is really listening to her, and she finishes ... and everybody laughs, everybody, and not this made-up kind of 'please like me' laugh but a real true surprising laugh where you laugh and surprise even yourself and make this ugly sound, [snorts] and I'm looking at MaryAnn smiling and everyone around her doing this real, surprising laughter and I'm thinking My God ... she's mine ...

So I'm thinking this standing on the ripped-up kitchen floor MaryAnn standing very close to me, she leans in even closer and she says: You're full of shit. And that is so cheap! She's always doing that shit metaphor with me because of my job and it's not my fault it's my job it's just my job, I was gonna be an engineer I was. But I'm not! But she's always doing that shit metaphor, you're full of shit, you suck shit, you eat shit, it is so cheap. But it pushes my BUTTON! So I leave, I'm late, I leave. Get in the car put on my YOU CAN DO IT positive thinking tape I got from group and I HATE THAT GUY'S VOICE: 'You can do it. You can do it. You can so do it.' But it sort of does the trick and re-channels my anger. Get to work everything's pretty much as per normal. Tom's telling lightbulb jokes out the window. Brenda's on the phone to an elevator repair company. But then things take a turn for the better: Andrew called in sick! Then, I'm standing by my desk Millard comes over to me, gives me one of these: [*hits himself in the shoulder with his fist*]. One of these: [*again*]. And that is just as ... that's better than a hug [*again*] cause you can still feel it later. Throughout the day he gives me several of these. Five-thirty comes Millard comes out of his office over to me at my desk says:

'You wanna go for a brew?'

'YES ... yeah sure okay.'

We go to the pub next door. I just have coffee cause I'm off the booze then but he has beer and I'm thinking if anybody walked in now who didn't know us they'd look over and say:

'Oh yeah a couple of buddies out for a drink after work one guy having coffee one guy having beer buddy must be on the wagon.'

They wouldn't even know the truth.

And Millard is really talking to me. He's asking me questions about myself.

He's asking me where I went to school:

'Where'd you go to school?'

He's asking me about my parents:

'Are your parents still living?'

He's asking me what's my favourite ballteam:

'What's your favourite—'

We got the same favourite ballteam! And not the local guys either, these other guys from away who nobody else even likes.

He tells me a dirty joke! (Which I won't repeat.)

Seven-thirty we pile into our cars, I get in mine he gets in his. Driving along get to my neighbourhood and I think Yes I am glad I am paying these high property taxes because this is a nice neighbourhood. I look in my rear-view mirror, and behind me, is my boss, coming to dinner, at my house.

Now I don't know if I just knew this cause sometimes you think back on something and you think Oh yeah I knew that, or if I knew because the floodlights weren't on the house like I asked.

[VICTOR *snaps his fingers, stage lights out. In the black:*]

So it's all dark. I get out of the car. Millard comes up to me:

'Wasn't your wife expecting us ha ha.'

I go in the house, Millard right behind me, walk in the kitchen, turn on the light.

[VICTOR *now uses the small clamp lamp to illuminate either his face or areas of the room he is describing*]

OH YES MaryAnn's got the tiles down. Thank you MaryAnn. But instead of black tile white tile black tile white tile black tile white tile she started with the black tiles and when she ran out of black tiles she started with the white tiles. She's got all the black tiles together and all the white tiles together. FABULOUS!

Noise in the living room. Go in the living room. Millard right behind me. And there's MaryAnn. And this is what she's wearing:

big black boots up to here ... no, higher, here, rubber panties, no bra no shirt no nothing, a leather mask that covers her whole head with a zipper for the mouth and in her hand she's got this piece of hose and she sort of flicks it at me like: Get Lost! Sitting in the easy chair by the teevee all tied up and wearing a diaper is ... ANDREW!

'Hey Sport, join the p-p-party!'

MaryAnn looks at Millard gives him one of these:

[*calling with his index finger*] c'meres,

I look at Millard he's got this zombie-Christmas-morning look on his face he looks at MaryAnn and says:

'VERONICA?'

She says to Millard:

'Call me Mommy you bastard.'

Like I need this.

I leave.

Get a room in a motel for the night, go into work the next day feeling like a real jerk, Andrew called in 'sick' again, Millard's not there didn't even call in doesn't have to owns the place. Two o'clock phone call comes, for me, it's MaryAnn:

'Please make other arrangements for the rest of your life.' Click. Buzzz. Two-thirty, phone call comes, for me, it's Millard's lawyer, and he says:

'Mister Millard would be interested in sitting down having a meeting with you to discuss the possibility of purchasing your house.'

He wants to buy my house.

He wants to buy my house.

He wants to …

He wants to buy my house.

And I think about this.

[VICTOR *spins the clamp lamp by the cord in wide circles over his head*]

And I think about it and I think about it and I think about it I think about it I think about it …

[*He catches the light and brings it to rest on his face*]

And I think about it and I think:

Hey, my boss, with my wife, in my house, hey, that kinda connection, that kinda connection, it's just a matter of time before it's:

[VICTOR *turns off the clamp lamp and snaps his fingers. Stage lights up full*]

'Hey Jimbo how ya doin! We won last night eh, pretty good. Listen anything you need? Look I'll call ya tomorrow, see ya Friday, wanna go for breakfast? Anything you need? Need a lift? Need some cash? Need a wife? Need a house? The shirt off my back? A pound of flesh perhaps!'

[VICTOR *snaps his fingers. Black. Throughout the following, spot up very slowly on* VICTOR *in the chair*]

A man and a woman were destined to meet and fall in love. They were supposed to meet while both were working in the mailroom of a large publishing company but due to an accident of fate this never happened. Instead the man secured a job behind the counter in a bookstore and the woman secured a job in a library. And even though the library was directly across the street from the bookstore and the bookstore was directly across the street from the library so severe and so serious was this accident of fate that in twenty-five years neither chanced to glance so much as the back of the other's head.

For a time both the man and the woman felt that something was missing in their lives but then they decided that this was just the feeling of being human.

Then one day the man decides what he needs in his life is a place of his own. So, he calls up a real-estate agent and makes plans to see a 'lovely little house' by the lake at twelve o'clock on Wednesday afternoon.

And one day the woman decides what she needs in her life is a place of her own. So, she calls up a real-estate agent and makes plans to see a 'lovely little house' by the lake at twelve-thirty on Wednesday afternoon.

And since the man was always late and the woman was always early they both arrive at the same time.

And they stand beside one another, nervous, strangers, until they are introduced by the real-estate agent, and as they shake hands and look into one another's eyes, they both become filled with all the experiences they had been destined to have:

five summers by the ocean, a year in Spain, the fat grey cat, the funny blue car, the antique bookcase, the wooden shutters, the ivy on the porch, the mornings over tea, the fear of heights, the red wine stain on the white dress, the terrible fight about the girl down the road ... on and on and more and more until the man and the woman become so filled with love that they then and there in the 'lovely little house' by the lake, they then and there, explode.

[*Black. In the black:*]

But as the real-estate agent will tell you:

'Oh it was a glorious explosion.'

[**VICTOR** *snaps his fingers. Stage lights up full*]

This is last week. I go to group. They're playing Word of the Week and God I hate Word of the Week … Gets to me, I say, 'Hey: my mother is possessed by the devil, my father is the saddest man in the world, my sister is in love with a dog, the one I love does not love me and I got no place to live.'

Mister 'Call-Me-Joe' (and I will not: call him Joe) he says:

'Hey Victor man we're playing Word of the Week right now alright?'

Alright, I sit down I shut up I don't say another word all night.

After everybody's sitting around talking about who's going for coffee. I leave. I can hear Mister 'Call-Me-Joe' (and I don't have to say it again):

'Hey Vic!'

Uh uh. I leave. And I walk out of that place with the walk of a man who is not coming back.

I'm sitting at Dinny's having my sixth cup of coffee this girl I don't know comes in sits at my booth. She's got a book, she says: mind if I read out loud? I go: WHA? She thinks that's 'yes' she starts reading. After a couple of pages she gets bored and stops. She's looking at me she

says: smoking is bad for you. I say: LEAK THAT TO
THE MEDIA!

Then we start talking and she tells me about her life
and that she's Scottish and then she starts to cry cause she
does have a pretty bad life so I play the bagpipes on my
throat which is something I do and she likes that cause
she's Scottish right. We talk some more and all of a
sudden I think, Hey she's a stranger right, a perfect
stranger right, perfect.

So I say to her:

'Hey you're a stranger right, a perfect stranger right,
perfect. I'm gonna tell you this and ask you something
and whatever you tell me I'll go by that.'

So I tell her:

'My mother is possessed by the devil, my father is the
saddest man in the world, my sister is in love with a dog,
the one I love does not love me and I got no place to live.
What should I do?'

Now she doesn't just jump in with some answer like:
'Join the Y!' No. She THINKS about it. And you can tell
that she's thinking about it cause she gets that look of a
wrinkled-up forehead and staring off at a spot that isn't
there. They are putting the chairs on the tables at Dinny's
she's still thinking. We gotta leave, we're walking on the
street she's still thinking about it. Walking down by the
ravine, she's still thinking. We gotta go back to her place
which is this sewer by the highway, well it's more like a

tunnel ... no, no, it's a sewer. So we're sitting there in the mouth of her sewer watching the trucks go by on the highway she's still thinking about it. Finally the sun's about to come up she gets up walks back to the middle of the sewer looks at me she's got this smile, she's gonna tell me what I should do. But then her smile that she's smiling keeps getting bigger across her whole face and it doesn't stop on her face, it keeps going right off her face, growing and growing and growing and fills up the whole inside of the sewer. Then, this smile it turns inside out and from inside the smile walk out all these people: MaryAnn, Millard, Andrew, Doris, my sister, my mother, my father, Darlene, Brenda, Tom, Dave the bishop, people, people, people, all the people I know and they are all wearing this smile of this girl and they are all smiling this smile at me. *Then*, every one of these people turn into birds. Every different kind of bird. Normal little brown birds, pigeons, bluebirds, parrots, eagles, birds of extinction, birds from storybooks, every different kind of bird, and then all these birds they come over to me and put their claws in me—but not in my skin! just in my clothes, in my jacket, in my pants, in my shoes, in my hair a little bit but not too hard ... I've got a million wings, and then all these birds they lift me up and fly me right out of the sewer out over the highway over houses over trees over the MOUNTAINS over the OCEAN far far away to this secret field that nobody knows exists—well some people know it but it's very hard to get to—and they drop me down in the middle of this field and I fall asleep and I have this dream:

[VICTOR *picks up the clamp lamp, snaps his fingers, stage lights out, clamp lamp on*]

We're not in the theatre. We're not in the building. We're in this dream. And we're on a bus. Going north. To ... Wadawhichawawa. (Wadawhichawawa!) It's very far north and we never been there before and we don't know anybody there and that's why we're going. It's night, dark, those little bus lights are on, some people are reading, some people are looking out the window, at the highway going by, trees moving, stars in the moonlight, animal eyes in the woods, dark, quiet. Then that woman at the front, in the blue sweater, the one from the pee break who bought the egg salad sandwich, she starts singing this song and we don't know it but we all start singing it too ... well if we sing it I guess we know it ...

[*sings*] *Well I'm coming by tomorrow with a hacksaw and a hammer*

*Gonna build a little place for you and me*

*Be just the way we like it and we'll make sure that it's sturdy*

*Gonna last a long long time for you and me.*

*And then that sunny morning we will move into our castle*

*Gonna keep the outside world from you and me*

*And we'll wake up every morning with our arms around each other and we'll walk into our kitchen and we'll hold our cups of coffee and we'll look out of our window and how oh so very happy we will be*

*We will be*

*And how oh so very happy we will be, be, be*

*be*


[**VICTOR** *slowly holds up his thumb and forefinger, he brings them together. Black*]

# HUMANS

## Contents

*for Tara MacDonald*

## List for a Lunenburg Bride

Microwaves, wedding presents, wicker chairs, wall-to-wall polyester carpeting, big teevees in wooden cabinets, country music, high shoes and tight belts, ex-husbands, step-children, new boyfriends, rum and Coke, dried flowers, traditional crystal, new cars, French braids, fun earrings, instant coffee, egg salad, wooden hugs, routine, suspicion, jealousy, strapless dresses, knee-highs, church halls, lucky numbers, process cheese, biorhythms, Kool-Aid, Jell-o, prayers and blessings in gold on plates over stoves on walls in kitchens, white bread, brushed velvet wallpaper, rock and roll, the Canadian flag, the American dream, lacquered plaques, oversized beer cans, lottery tickets, bingo dappers, ultra-mild ultra-slim menthol cigarettes, electric knives, barbequed beef, satellite dishes, a different ornament for the tree every year, belief in advertising, obsession with weight, an almost hysterical compulsion for action smothered by inertia. ■

## Harold

Harold is an old man who goes to the theatre. He does not hear very well and his eyes are bad. Mostly he likes the people. He always sits at the front and claps in all the wrong places and yells out Marxist slogans during tender moments and calls the actors by their real names. (Once he went to see a play where at one point a watermelon would roll out and surprise the audience, and he went back several times so that just before the watermelon would roll out he could yell: 'Here comes the watermelon!' Things like that.) Most people suffer Harold grudgingly and roll their eyes when they see him in line, but when he dies there will be a big award named after him: and everyone will want to win it. ∎

*Romeo's Sister*
*(for John Alcorn)*

Romeo lives with his sister and her two kids and never worked a day in his life. They've got a house full of junk and Romeo's got a lock on his bedroom door. He doesn't read, doesn't watch the teevee, he just locks the door and looks at himself in the mirror.

He's not even handsome.

Every morning he gets up and eats three fried eggs with white burnt toast and sweet strawberry jam. He has two cups of weak tea with two teaspoons of sugar and then leaves heading down the road past the store and then over the hill to the track.

Last Friday Romeo calls his sister from the track.

He says: 'How much cash you got?'

She says: 'On me?'

He says: 'No altogether.'

She says: 'Seven hundred.'

He says: 'With your vacation money.'

She hesitates. 'A thousand?'

He says: 'Get it and meet me here in half an hour.' ▸

And she does and he loses it all on one race.

She shows him she's still got a twenty in her shoe and they buy beer and hotdogs and put the last ten dollars on Daisy Chain to Show in the Eighth at odds of 10 to 1 and they lose.

On the way home they walk through the park and Romeo tells his sister a story about hummingbirds and they sit on the bench and they watch the sun go down behind the mall and Romeo's sister forgets all about her vacation because how could it be a vacation without Romeo.

(His real name is Dave but his sister calls him Romeo.) ■

## *Dripping Wet and Hissing at the Window*

Since the girl had been back she had not been sleeping for fear of dreaming. She had just returned from her aunt's house in the city. While there she had: after a week settled down; after two: slept soundly; after three: spent her days absorbed in games with the children who lived downstairs. But now back, her father just down the hall, she could only remember how his arms moved so easily that morning as he picked each of the small bags up as she stood back watching near the climbing tree, the sound of stones in water and the sudden realization ...

Again tonight she cried, while down the hall her father would once again be paid a visit in his dreams by that green-eyed kitten. ■

## Fiddle in a Field of Fire

I ngrid taught mathematics at a private school for boys outside the city. She lived alone in a small wooden cottage just past the church. Every day she would walk to school past the dry cleaners down the path by the American's summer place and over the narrow bridge across the deep, dark, dangerous ravine. Every day she would stop on the bridge and look down into the ravine and think: 'How deep, how dark, how dangerous.' Every day she would approach the school with her head down and enter her classroom and Ingrid would sit and look out over the sea of bobbing heads and floating pencils, all those privileged boys who would become privileged men and marry women and give them easy lives. If she hadn't been a Christian she would surely have hated them.

The Janitor at the school was a man of forty-five. He was tall and thin and spoke in short quiet sentences. Near the end of the school year the Janitor began courting Ingrid. He would leave poetic verses ➤

on her blackboard (he would find these in dusty books in the school library). He would leave roses on her doorstep (he would buy these from the curious woman at the flower store). He would put candy in the drawers of her desk (and sometimes as he bent down there he would place his face on her chair and think of her lovely hands). All of this and yet Ingrid would not speak to the Janitor. 'He's a Janitor,' thought Ingrid, 'a Janitor.' Finally one Sunday evening the Janitor went to Ingrid's house and stood on the path leading up to her door. Ingrid noticed him from the window upstairs at 6:15, standing there holding his hat in front of him like a helmet. At 7:00 he began to sing 'You're My Thrill' over and over in a high windy voice. By 9:30 Ingrid decided she must do something or the neighbours would surely call the police (if they hadn't already). She opened the door and said: 'What do you want?'

The Janitor lifted his head and quietly said: 'What can I do to make you see me?'

Ingrid did not take a moment to think and said: 'Throw five boys off the bridge.'

She slammed the door and withdrew into her ➤

cottage. At 10:10 when she ventured to the window the Janitor was gone. Ingrid went to bed and dreamed of a man playing a fiddle in a field of fire. The next day school was cancelled and shortly thereafter Ingrid left her job and took an apartment in the city in a building near the prison where she visits the Janitor. Two hours twice a week. ∎

## Somebody (to 1984)

Circuses, toy stores, wine bottles, carpeting, teevee, being carried, my sister's hair, my mother's uniform, my father's headache, Pepsi, french fries, Hallowe'en, swimming, girls, boys, mathematics, the journey toward eliminating mathematics from my reality, unidentified flying objects, death, Richie Rich, Red Skelton, Cheez Whiz, masturbation, wine bottles, pretending, being disappointed, 'Laugh-In,' Kraft Dinner, fear of heights, desire to fly, emergency rooms, not liking my name, not liking my nose, McDonald's, the longing for and great appreciation of summer, pizza, Norman Lear, lemon gin, Nestlé Instant Breakfast, sperm, Wide Legs, suicidal tendencies, James Taylor, *The Mountain and the Valley*, warm beer in ravines, paranoia, marijuana, religion, car keys, grey Levi-cords, leg sex, French toast, disco, not understanding the dances, warm beer, driving fast, emergency rooms, *MAD* magazine, camping, coming to terms with having no concept of 'nature,' leaving home, university, cold beer, the ➤

concept of 'Canada,' the concept of 'concept,' finding sex, appreciating the social value of university, Plato's *The Last Days of Socrates,* failing philosophy, finding sex, the journey toward forgetting about television as anything but a fear of experience, finding sex, finding sex, *The Catcher in the Rye* (finally), poverty, bad habits, concern about finding sex, questioning mortality, Shirley MacLaine, understanding the danger of fame, good parties, AIDS, a million questions, no answers, the concept of 'personal history,' the questioning of the reality of the possibility of the existence of a personal future, my sister's hair, being carried, teevee, carpeting, wine bottles, toy stores, circuses. ∎

## The Stupid Boyfriend

There was a woman who had a dog. The woman and the dog lived alone. The woman thought of herself as an average sort of person (and unfortunately this was reflected in her choice of lovers) but when the woman thought of the dog she felt for sure he was not an average dog at all, for this was a dog who laughed. When the dog was happy (which was most of the time) he would smile and laugh just like a human. Of course it was different than a human smile or laugh because the smile and laugh came from the mouth and the voice of a dog. Some people, if they didn't want to believe in the laughing, could easily pass it off as a quirk or the result of some accident. Then the woman met a man and they exchanged words of love and because it was the most convenient thing the man moved in with the woman and the dog. When the man met the dog he too knew that the dog was not an average dog and he knew that the dog was laughing and he knew that the dog was laughing at him. (This man was the sort of person ➤

who knew that when he walked into a room and people stopped talking it was because they were talking about him, or if he was on a bus and little girls giggled behind him it was because of his hair.) After a time the man convinced the woman to give the dog away, to a family who lived outside the city. This was a very sad thing. Sad because away from the woman the dog stopped smiling and laughing and very sad because the dog, like most people, had no opinion about the man whatsoever. ■

## Are You There?

Henry died suddenly.

Henry's brother was given the task of calling a woman in another city who loved Henry very much for many years. Henry's brother though, being a soft and timid sort of person, could not bring himself to make the call. Each day he would wake up and think: 'Yes today I will call her and tell her of Henry's demise.' But as each day moved forward he found many things to do which were not the phone call and then it would be night and just too late.

This went on for many days which became months. One day almost a year after the funeral there was a knock on Henry's brother's door. It was the woman who loved Henry.

She said: 'I've quit my job and sold my house and left my husband to come and be with Henry.'

Henry's brother was stunned and *without thinking* said: 'Henry moved to Florida.'

The woman asked him: 'Where in Florida?'

Henry's brother said he did not have an: 'exact ➤

address.'

The woman asked him: 'Roughly?'

Henry's brother said: 'Roughly Miami.'

And then the woman was gone.

For two months Henry's brother felt very bad for having lied to the woman but then one afternoon as he was chewing on the nail of his little finger and staring out the window at cars whizzing by through slush he remembered one winter many years ago when he and Henry and the woman were sitting in a café in Calgary and the woman said: 'Jesus-god I hate the cold.'

Suddenly Henry's brother felt better and even responsible for helping the woman to a much greater happiness.

Less than a week later the telephone rang. It was the woman. She told him that after much searching she had found Henry and they were to be married in the spring ... The last thing he remembered was the telephone hitting his foot and a woman's voice far away. ■

*April 11*

There were three sheep in a field. They were very happy in this field together and played games and made up songs about how wonderful it was to be three sheep in a field unbothered by the rest of the world. They would talk about how rude and cruel the other animals were and how *fortunate* they were: first, because they were sheep and second, because they were three sheep together. The first sheep was an arrogant and bossy sort of sheep, the second sheep was nervous and made jokes about itself and the third sheep was the quiet sheep who was thoughtful and mostly just smiled and nodded and did what was expected.

Then on April 9 the third sheep while walking alone came across a tiger sticking its head through the slats on the fence which separated the sheep's land from the rest of the world. The tiger had a friendly face and asked the sheep to come and play. The sheep said nothing but watched the tiger, at first thinking of danger but then noticing there was something ►

about the tiger which was sad, a kind of sad the sheep remembered the way one might remember a history lesson. Since it was getting dark the third sheep made its way home thinking all the while about what it might be like to play with a tiger. Later when the three sheep were together the third sheep asked the first and second sheep about tigers.

The first sheep said: 'Tigers eat sheep.'

The second sheep said: 'If I wasn't a sheep I would want to be a tiger.'

The next day, April 10, the third sheep once again wandered to the spot in the fence where the day before it had seen the tiger. The sheep poked its nose through the fence and smelled for the tiger then wandered down to that secret part of the field where the fence opened just enough for a sheep to get out and *without even stopping to think* the third sheep squeezed out into the rest of the world. For many hours the sheep wandered through the fields and forests it had never known existed, and then came upon the tiger asleep under a huge glorious tree. The third sheep then lay down with the tiger and fell asleep. ➤

In the morning the tiger woke and kissed the third sheep and told the sheep all about humans. ∎

## His Smell That Room Her Green Dress

There was a man who was very jealous. This man was so jealous that whenever another man would gaze even slightly upon his wife while looking past her he would go into a red rage, swearing and flaring his nostrils. This was very hard on the wife who was a social person and liked to meet new people, but she loved the man and constantly assured him that it was only him for her. One of the things the wife loved about the man was a particular smell he had, like danger mixed with nature. There were many other things that the woman loved about the man but this was one particular special thing. And when he was jealous the woman would push her face into her husband's neck and breathe deeply and think how much she loved him.

The woman had a job which required her to travel to other cities and sleep in hotel rooms. A weekend came where the woman had to go to an important meeting far away. She was going with a young man who worked in her office. ➤

The jealous man's wife sat beside him on the bed, her suitcase by the door, and she pressed her face into his neck and then she left. But as soon as the door was closed he started imagining everything: the hotel room the bed the butterscotch blankets and carpets and curtains the television on the small round table the large mirror the empty drawers the desk by the window the writing paper her green dress the bed the young man in the soft chair the drinks his blue eyes his jacket off (he leans over she laughs they fall back) her green dress. On and on and over and over no matter how he tried to change the events or think of something else: he could not.

In her hotel room the woman could not explain it—the young man's eyes, his jacket off and he leans over and they're kissing and her green dress … and there was that smell, so strong, so close, as if he was right there with them in that room. ∎

*Lake*

Harold Broomfield left today. No note has been found. From what we can gather he packed one small black nylon overnight bag with two pairs of blue jeans, a white shirt, a few pairs of socks, some underwear and a dictionary (since the dictionary from Mr. Broomfield's den is missing). Also he might have taken that picture of Joey from the hallway but Mrs. Broomfield can't remember if she had it put away last summer with the rest of Joey's things. A man who works at the gas station across from the bus terminal thinks he might have seen Harold get on the out-of-town-two-o'clock which makes sense since Harold's biology teacher said he wasn't in class (which began at 1:45).

Now the rest is in my imagination but in my imagination Harold is on the bus and pretending to be reading the dictionary and as the bus passes the lake he is pretending he has found the saddest word.

Joey wanted to be an astronaut. ➤

(The police around Cape Canaveral have been notified to be on the lookout for a twelve-year-old with a big book and his older brother's eyes.) ∎

## List #3 (for a 50th Anniversary)

Toaster. Teevee. Electric kettle. Sofa. Matching loveseat, chair and ottoman. Kitchen table and four chairs. Bed. Clock radio. 195,000 knick-knacks … Keepsakes. (Knick-knacks, keepsakes, knick-knacks, keepsakes etc.) Night-table. Piano. Playing cards. China cabinet. Plates and bowls and forks and knives and cups and saucers and pots and pans and spoons. Three suitcases. Two suits, four shirts, seven undershirts, five pairs of socks, six pairs of underwear, two pairs of pyjamas, a brown sweater, a hat, a winter coat, a spring jacket, boots and two pairs of shoes. Five dresses, a blue sweater, a dozen pairs of hose, underwear and so on, three hats, two purses, a winter coat, a spring jacket and two pairs of shoes. Three rugs. A laundry basket. A fern. The first half of a set of encyclopedias. Seven hundred and fifty dollars set aside for the first funeral and whatever's in the fridge. ∎

*Words*

Two men met. One man spoke only French and one man spoke only English. However before they had a chance to find this out many plans had been made between the two from across the room. When they got outside the bar, that is when they realized they could not communicate with words. At first they both were startled, neither having been in this position before, but as they walked they both talked nervously, even though both understood that the other could not understand. The English man watched the French man and how he moved his face and hands, the French man watched the English man and how he smiled. When they got back to the English man's apartment and into his bed mouths and fingers took the place of words and this was very good.

In the morning each man was far more comfortable than he had ever been before with a stranger at the table because they both knew words were impossible and thus unnecessary, and this put the two ➤

men very much at ease. After three months together the men began to pick up each other's language. The French man noticed how the English man's words formed prudish ideas, the English man noticed how the French man's words formed bitter ideas. But it was too late now that they had fallen in love and so they made a rule that everything and anything could pass between them as long as there were no words involved. ■

## The Canadian Widow

First we had a Chrysler. Then a red Chevrolet station-wagon we called 'Rusty' but it wasn't really rusty though, we named it after a chicken in a bag on a show the kids watched. Then another Chrysler. A Firebird. Then a Valiant, light green. A blue Dodge truck. A silver Datsun (never ran right). A blue Plymouth. A black Chrysler, mid-sized. (And whenever he drove he had one arm on the wheel, and if it was winter, one arm on the door, and if it was summer, one arm out the window, and always, every year, there'd be one evening the end of June he'd come in after being out in the car all day and he'd have a really bad burn on just his left arm and I'd put some Noxzema on it and we'd be lying in bed and I'd be doing my puzzle and he'd be moving his arm at the elbow, in and out, in and out, and he'd say: 'A sunburn always makes me feel like a boy.') ■

*A Story with a Moral*
*(for Veronica MacDonald)*

Once there was a man who was in a very bad mood. He woke up in the morning and even though the sun was shining all he saw was rain, and even though the cat was purring and rubbing his legs he kicked it, when he left the house he trampled all the violets he had so carefully planted that spring, when he got to work he sent nasty anonymous messages to his co-workers on his computer, he jammed the photocopier, he didn't recycle his Styrofoam cups, he put a plastic fork in the microwave and told Debbie in accounting she had 'body odour.' On the way home he drove quickly through puddles trying to splash pedestrians and once there kept burning fish sticks in the oven until after 3:00 A.M. to set off the smoke detector and drive the neighbours crazy. Then he went to bed and thought: 'Well at least today is over and I will feel better tomorrow.'

But tomorrow came and he did not feel better at all. He kicked the cat, he trampled the violets, he sent nasty anonymous messages, he told Debbie in ➤

accounting she was 'fat,' he sped through puddles and kept fish sticks burning until dawn. And the next day and the next day and the next day were worse and worse and worse. Crushed violets, angry co-workers, a hardening Debbie, confused pedestrians, crazed neighbours.

And so the man, wishing for violets and terribly tired of rain, went to see a doctor. The doctor told the man that in order to get out of his very bad mood he would have to climb a mountain and sing a song.

The man asked the doctor, 'Which mountain? What song?'

'That,' said the doctor, 'is entirely Sir up to you.'

The next day the man spoke to some people who knew some people who knew something about the difference between mountains and hills and it was simple enough to find an easily climbed mountain in that relatively flat province.

But a song?

The man knew no one who knew anything at all about songs. The next morning he went to the door of his neighbour who he had heard from time to time playing records but the neighbour could see it was ➤

the nuisance next door and would not answer the bell. And all day long at work when he would approach someone to ask about songs (the man at the desk, the woman in the lunch room) everyone would avoid or ignore him. The man became slightly panicked that he might never find a song to sing and might never feel better again. Finally the woman who made coffee took pity on him and told him that upstairs in accounting he should talk to Debbie, the girl in the choir.

The man had not even said a word, he had merely approached Debbie's desk and leaned down, barely even taking her attention when she hit him so hard with a stack of files that he stumbled backwards into a water cooler, through a plate-glass window and plummeted fifteen storeys to his death in the street below.

And the moral of the story is: Learn a Song. ■